RELIGION

LIFE IN ANCIENT EGYPT

RELIGION

BY

KATHRYN HINDS

**Marshall Cavendish
Benchmark**
New York

To Owen

The author and publisher wish to specially thank J. Brett McClain of the Oriental Institute of the University of Chicago for his invaluable help in reviewing the manuscript.

MARSHALL CAVENDISH BENCHMARK 99 WHITE PLAINS ROAD TARRYTOWN, NEW YORK 10591-9001
www.marshallcavendish.us

LIBRARY OF CONGRESS CATALOGING-IN-PUBLICATION DATA: Hinds, Kathryn, 1962- Religion / by Kathryn Hinds. p. cm. — (Life in ancient Egypt) Summary: "Describes the role of religion in ancient Egypt during the New Kingdom period, from about 1550 BCE to about 1070 BCE, including the diverse gods and goddesses the people worshipped, their creation myths, and the role of the priesthood"—Provided by publisher. Includes bibliographical references and index. ISBN-13: 978-0-7614-2186-3 ISBN-10: 0-7614-2186-6 1. Egypt—Religion—Juvenile literature. 2. Egypt—History— New Kingdom, ca. 1550-ca. 1070 B.C.—Juvenile literature. I. Title. II. Series: Hinds, Kathryn, 1962- Life in ancient Egypt. BL2441.3H56 2006   299'.31—dc22   2006011086

EDITOR: Joyce Stanton   EDITORIAL DIRECTOR: Michelle Bisson
ART DIRECTOR: Anahid Hamparian   SERIES DESIGNER: Michael Nelson

Images provided by Rose Corbett Gordon, Art Editor, Mystic CT, from the following sources:
Cover: The Art Archive/Dagli Orti   Back cover: Ann Ronan Picture Library/HIP/The Image Works Pages i, 30: Borromeo/Art Resource NY; page iii: Werner Forman/Art Resource NY; pages iv, vi, 61: The Art Archive/Bibliothèque Musée du Louvre/Dagli Orti; page viii: Scala/Art Resource, NY; pages 3, 39, 40, 50, 54, 60: Erich Lessing/Art Resource, NY; pages 4, 18: Gianni Dagli Orti/Corbis; pages 5, 31: The Art Archive/Egyptian Museum Turin/Dagli Orti; pages 7, 32: The Art Archive/Musée du Louvre Paris/Dagli Orti; pages 8, 58: CM Dixon/HIP/The Image Works; pages 10, 17, 20, 49, 52: The Art Archive/Dagli Orti; page 12: Mary Evans Picture Library; page 13: Christie's Images/Corbis; page 15: Charles Walker/Topfoto/The Image Works; page 16: Getty/Bridgeman Art Library; page 22: Sandro Vannini/ Corbis; page 24: Louvre, Paris/Peter Willi/Bridgeman Art Library; page 26: The Art Archive/Egyptian Museum Cairo/Dagli Orti(A); page 27: Werner Forman/Topham/The Image Works; page 28: National Geographic/Getty Images; page 34: Bridgeman Art Library/ Getty Images; page 36: North Wind Picture Archives; page 37: Werner Forman/Egyptian Museum Cairo/The Image Works; page 41: Giraudon/Art Resource, NY; page 43: AAAC/Topham/The Image Works; page 44: Getty Images; page 46: The British Museum/Topham-HIP/The Image Works; page 47: The Art Archive/Egyptian Museum Cairo/Dagli Orti; page 51: E. Strouhal/Werner Forman Archive/Art Resource, NY; page 57: Werner Forman/Topham/The Image Works; page 59: Egyptian National Museum Cairo/Giraudon/Bridgeman Art Library.

Printed in China
135642

front cover: A priest, dressed in a ceremonial leopard skin, raises an offering bowl.
half-title page: A baboon, from an ancient Egyptian wall painting. Baboons were among the several animals ancient Egyptians held sacred.
title page: This illustration from a book of the afterlife shows a man praying to Anubis, the god of mummification and funerals.
page vi: Sacred animals—a lion, a heron, and a falcon—from a wall painting in the tomb of Queen Nefertari
back cover: Thoth, the ibis-headed god of wisdom and writing, dips a pen into the ink on his scribe's palette.

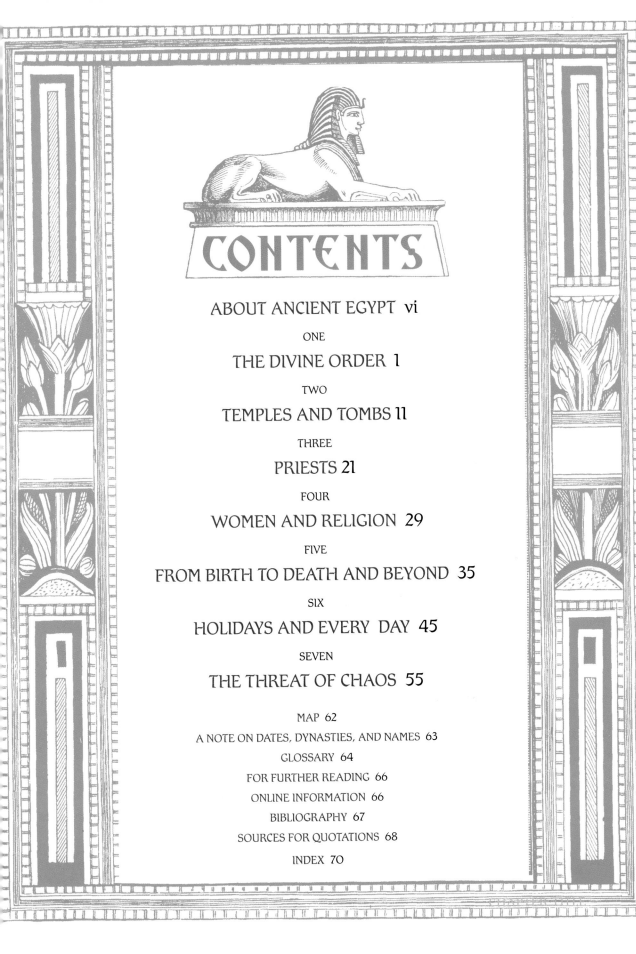

CONTENTS

ABOUT ANCIENT EGYPT

When we think about ancient Egypt, magnificent images immediately come to mind: the pyramids, the Sphinx, the golden funeral mask of "King Tut," colossal statues of mighty kings. Our imaginations are full of mummies and tombs, hieroglyphic symbols and animal-headed goddesses and gods. Most of us, however, don't often give much thought to the people of ancient Egypt and how they lived their everyday lives. Where would we even start?

Ancient Egyptian history is vast—about three thousand years long, in fact, from the first known pharaoh (Aha, also called Menes) to the last independent ruler (Cleopatra VII). During this span of time, Egyptian society and culture naturally underwent many changes. So to make it easier to get to know the people of ancient Egypt, this series of books focuses on a smaller chunk of history, the period known as the New Kingdom, from about 1550 to about 1070 BCE. This was the era of ancient Egypt's greatest power and the time of some of its most famous pharaohs, or rulers: Hatshepsut, Thutmose III, Amenhotep III, Akhenaten, Tutankhamen, Ramses II.

During the New Kingdom, Egypt—or Kemet ("The Black Land"), as its people called it—was the dominant force in the Mediterranean world. The pharaohs controlled territory from Syria to what is now Sudan, and their influence stretched to Asia Minor and Mesopotamia. Yet no matter how wide their connections, the Egyptians maintained a unique culture with its own writing, artistic style, religion, type of government, and social organization. And always at the center of life was the Nile River, which made Egypt a long, narrow oasis of greenery in the midst of the desert.

In this book you will learn about the role of religion in ancient Egypt. You will meet priests and priestesses, and you will also see how people in other walks of life related to the gods and goddesses. You will visit temples, shrines, and tombs. You will learn how religious beliefs affected people's daily lives and their hopes for the afterlife. So step back into history, to a time even before the splendors of ancient Greece and Rome. Welcome to life in ancient Egypt!

A variety of systems of dating have been used by different cultures throughout history. Many historians now prefer to use BCE (Before Common Era) and CE (Common Era) instead of BC (Before Christ) and AD (Anno Domini), out of respect for the diversity of the world's peoples.

ONE

THE DIVINE ORDER

To understand anything about the ancient Egyptians—including their religion—we must first understand the land they lived in. There was one thing, and one thing only, that made civilization possible in Egypt: the Nile River. It was almost the sole source of fresh water, for rain seldom fell. Beyond the narrow ribbon of land watered by the Nile lay nothing but desert, except for a few scattered oases.

Every year the Nile's level rose, and the surrounding land was submerged under the river. When the waters receded again, they left ponds, canals, and irrigation ditches filled. The river also left behind a layer of rich silt that renewed the soil. Because of this, Egypt was one of the most fertile places in the ancient world, producing abundant crops.

The Egyptians' beliefs were colored by their relationship to the river and its annual flood. The ever-repeating pattern of the sea-

Opposite:
Maat, the goddess who personified truth and justice, also represented what ancient Egyptians valued most: order and balance.

1

sons—flood, growing season, harvest—was all-important. It was the earthly image of the divinely ordered universe. In human life as in nature, order and balance were the constant ideal. The Egyptians had a name for this ideal: *maat*. It stood for truth and justice, too, because these were also aspects of the divine order, the balance that allowed life to continue and to thrive. The opposite of *maat* was *isfet,* chaos—disorder, imbalance—and was to be avoided at all costs.

BEGINNINGS

"Before the sky evolved, before the earth evolved, before people evolved, before the gods were born, before death evolved," the creator was alone with Nu (or Nun), the cosmic waters. Nu was dark, infinite, and inert. Like the annual Nile flood, however, these waters eventually receded. A mound or hillock emerged from them, and on it landed the Benu Bird (later called the phoenix by the Greeks), a gigantic heron. It uttered a cry, the first sound, filling the world with "that which it had not known," and over the primeval mound, the sun rose for the first time.

The Benu Bird, as well as the mound itself, was identified with the god Atum, the "Complete One." Atum was also called "he who came into being of himself," who set all the rest of creation in motion. From his spit came the goddess Tefnut ("Moisture") and the god Shu ("Air"). They gave birth to Nut ("Sky") and her husband Geb ("Earth"). This pair then had two daughters, Isis and Nephthys, and two sons, Osiris and Seth. Atum and his descendants made up the deities known as the Ennead, or group of nine.

Sometimes Atum was replaced in the Ennead by the god Re (or Ra), "the god who came into being by himself, when he was king of humans and gods together," and sometimes the two gods were combined as Re-Atum. Re embodied the sun at its height, but he could take different forms and different names. In one myth, for

MULTIPLE MYTHS

The Egyptians prized not only order, but also tradition. Even while their culture was very stable, though, it was not unchanging. As new religious practices and beliefs developed over time, the Egyptians simply added them onto the old, traditional ones. Also, there were numerous local and regional variations in beliefs and practices. For these reasons, we find many differences and even contradictions in ancient Egyptian mythology—for example, different creation tales and varying explanations for the sun's nighttime disappearance. None of this seems to have bothered the Egyptians; they were able to embrace a diversity of beliefs. For instance, they might see one creation story as appropriate for certain occasions, and another version of the myth as more suited to other circumstances. They also had no problem with adding new deities to the ones they already worshipped, with combining two deities from different parts of the country, with seeing a single deity as having diverse characteristics, or with having several deities concerned with the same thing. There was no single book or scripture that told the Egyptians what to believe—but *maat* and tradition combined to guide them in their relationships with the deities and with each other.

Above: The sun god takes three forms in this painting: As Khepri, he rises between two trees, as Horakhty-Atum he rides on the back of a young calf, and as Re he takes the shape of a falcon-headed figure crowned with a sun disk.

Ptah, god of artisans, created both the divine and human worlds through his thoughts and words.

example, Re tells Isis, "At dawn, I am called Khepri [the scarab god]; at midday, Re; and in the evening, Atum." Most Egyptian sun gods were identified with Re in one form or another. His most famous image is probably that of the Great Sphinx of Giza, which was seen as an embodiment of Re-Horakhty, the sun on the horizon.

Atum and Re had a major center of worship in the city of Iunu (later known as On in the Bible and as Heliopolis to the Greeks). Not far away in Memphis, however, the chief god was Ptah, and so there he played the "starring" role in the creation story:

The gods who came into being as Ptah:
Ptah upon the Great Throne . . .
Ptah-Nun, the father who begot Atum . . .
Ptah-Naunet, the mother who bore Atum . . .
Ptah, the Great, that is the heart and tongue of the Ennead.

The priests of Memphis taught that Ptah existed before both Atum and Thoth, a god of wisdom and writing who was also regarded as a creator deity in some parts of Egypt. These two lived only because Ptah had thought of them and spoken their names. In fact, "every divine word came into being through that which the Heart of Ptah thought and the Tongue of Ptah commanded. Thus every kind of work and every handicraft, and everything done with the arms, and every motion of the legs and every action of all the limbs takes place through this command, which is conceived by the heart . . . and brought about by the tongue."

THE KING OF THE GODS

During the New Kingdom, one god rose to greater national importance than any other: Amen, the chief deity of Thebes. This city was the hometown of the first New Kingdom pharaohs, and it was they who elevated Amen to his supreme position. Amen's name meant "hidden," for he was ultimately unknowable. "He is hidden from the gods, and his aspect is unknown. He is farther than the sky, he is deeper than the Duat [the underworld]. No god knows his true appearance. . . . He is too secret to uncover his awesomeness, he is too great to investigate, too powerful to know."

Although it was said that Amen was hidden and unknowable, Egyptian artists portrayed him as a man in the prime of life. Here he stands protectively in front of the young pharaoh Tutankhamen.

Other Egyptian deities were identified with things in the visible world—the environment, animals, stars, weather, people, etc.—but not Amen. He was outside of nature. Therefore, he could be thought of as the ultimate creator of nature, who encompassed all the rest of the deities. As one hymn to Amen said, "The Ennead is combined in your body: your image is every god, joined in your person." Another hymn stated the idea that there was one ultimate divine being who could be seen as a combination of Amen, Re, and Ptah:

> Past knowing His nature as Amen, the hidden,
> He is Re in His features, in body is Ptah. . . .
> Since each move of His lips is most secret,
> gods carry out what He commands.

God's Word, it can kill or perpetuate,
life or death for all men unfolds by means of it,
And He opens His countenance as Re, Ptah, or Amen,
a trinity of unchanging forms.

Amen eventually was combined with Re to become Amen-Re. His priests taught that his city, Thebes, was the place where the entire universe was born. From his temple there, Amen-Re reigned as "Lord of Time who makes the years, rules the months, ordains nights and days."

THE MANY FACES OF THE DIVINE

Every Egyptian city and village had its local deities, and many of them were honored mainly in their home region. Others, though—like the Ennead, Amen, and Thoth—came to be worshipped throughout Egypt. A large number of goddesses and gods could take animal form as well as human form, or they might be thought of as having human bodies and animal heads. Following are some of the many deities the Egyptians worshipped.

Horus: There were actually two gods by this name. One was a god of the sun and sky, who often took the form of a falcon or falcon-headed man. The other, sometimes called Harpocrates (a Greek form of his name), was the son of Isis and Osiris and was one of the mythological first kings of Egypt. The ancient Egyptians, however, frequently regarded the two as being the same god. The reigning pharaoh, referred to as the Living Horus, was his embodiment on Earth.

Hathor: sometimes regarded as the daughter of Re; one of her titles was the Eye of Re. Other titles included the Golden One, the Lady of Song, Mistress of Maidens, and Lady of the Sycamore. She was a goddess of music, beauty, love, women, motherhood, childbirth, and the sky. Her sacred animal was the cow, and sycamore trees were special to her. Egyptian queens were closely identified with Hathor, and she was one of the most popular deities with people in all walks of life throughout Egyptian history.

Sekhmet: the wife of Ptah; sometimes regarded as a fierce form of Hathor. Like Hathor, she was called the Eye of Re. One of her roles was to devour the enemies of the sun and to help the king kill the enemies of Egypt. Her name means "The Powerful One," and she could both cause and cure illness. Sekhmet was usually portrayed as a woman with the head of a lioness.

Bast: Another goddess referred to as the Eye of Re, she could be thought of as a gentler form of Sekhmet. She was a goddess of music, dancing, motherhood, protection, and prosperity. Her sacred animal was the cat, and the center of her worship was the city of Bubastis in the Nile delta.

Anubis: a god of death, cemeteries, and embalming (mummification). Two of his most important titles were Lord of the Necropolis and He Who Belongs to the Mummy Wrappings. He took the form of a black jackal or other wild canine, or a man with a jackal's head.

Maat: the daughter of Re. She was the personification of the ideal of *maat*—truth, justice, balance, and order. She was represented as a woman wearing an ostrich feather on her head. The ostrich feather alone could also stand for her, and it was the hieroglyph for the word *truth*.

The much-loved goddess Hathor, in her cow form, watches over Pharaoh Ramses II as he journeys in a boat with a lotus-shaped prow.

Khnum, "The Molder," was held in particular honor in southern Egypt, where he was revered as the god who made humans from clay and gave them the breath of life.

Mut: the wife of Amen. She was a goddess of motherhood and protection. Her sacred animal was the vulture, and in her honor New Kingdom queens often wore a golden headdress made to look like vulture's wings.

Khonsu (or **Khons**): the son of Amen and Mut, a god of the moon, time, and healing.

Montu: a hawk-headed god connected with warfare and the sun.

Min: a god of the desert and of miners, hunters, travelers, and nomads.

Aten: the visible sun (the sun disk), and the sun's life-giving powers. Originally he was closely identified with Re and was portrayed in human form. Later he was shown in art as a sun disk with many rays, each ending in a small hand.

Nekhbet: a vulture goddess, guardian of Upper (southern) Egypt. She also assisted at the births of kings and gods.

Wadjet: a cobra goddess, guardian of Lower (northern) Egypt. Together with Nekhbet, she protected the pharaoh and symbolized his rule over all of Egypt.

Neit (or **Neith**): a very ancient goddess, connected with hunting, war, and the Nile Delta. A myth recorded in the city of Edfu told how she was the first being to emerge from the primeval waters.

She then uttered the name of the primeval mound, thereby bringing it into being. Next she created light and the first gods, and prophesied the birth of the sun. Once the sun rose for the first time, she turned the work of creation over to the ram-headed god **Khnum,** who used clay and his potter's wheel to make all living things. Eventually Khnum passed his creative powers on to the females of every species, while he kept the job of breathing the life force into everything born.

TWO

TEMPLES AND TOMBS

The world fears time, but time fears the pyramids," says an Arabic proverb. Indeed, by the New Kingdom, the pyramids were already nearly a thousand years old. They were objects of awe and reverence, to which many people made pilgrimages. For example, a man named Ahmose left behind graffiti commemorating his visit to the Step Pyramid of Saqqara; he wrote that to him the pyramid looked "as though heaven were within it." Most ancient Egyptian religious structures were meant to contain or represent "heaven," or at least a little bit of it. Whether houses for the great gods or for the honored dead, they were made of stone to last through the ages—to conquer time.

MANSIONS OF THE GODS

Egyptian temples were not like the houses of worship familiar to most people today. A temple was a god's "mansion" and, like any

Opposite:
Columns soar skyward in the temple of Amen at Karnak.

11

The temple of Horus in Edfu, southern Egypt, as it appeared in 1920. The painting gives an excellent view of the pylon, or monumental entryway. We can also see the open-air courtyard and the hypostyle hall.

private home, most of it was off-limits to the general public. Most private of all was the inner sanctuary, sometimes called the holy of holies. This windowless room was the heart of the temple. It housed the sacred statue of the god, and only the pharaoh and the highest-ranking priests had access to it.

An Egyptian temple generally had four basic parts: a pylon, or monumental gateway; an open-air courtyard with colonnades alongside; a wide hall with a roof supported by many pillars, often referred to as a hypostyle hall; and finally the sanctuary. Sometimes this plan is hard to see, though, because as a deity grew in importance, his or her temple grew in size and complexity. As a result, Egypt's most prestigious temples developed into sprawling compounds of many gateways, courtyards, buildings, and other features.

The enlargement and embellishment of temples was an ongoing process that could take place over generations or even centuries. This is very clear in the most famous and important New Kingdom temple, Karnak in Thebes, which was dedicated primarily to Amen. Ipet-isut was its Egyptian name—"the most select of places." It had its beginnings during the Middle Kingdom, when Amen was simply

SACRED SYMBOLISM

A great deal of symbolism was involved in the architecture of the mansions of the gods. The symbolism began with the wall that surrounded the holy precincts, setting them apart from the outside world. This wall, or the outer pylons, typically showed the king defeating his enemies, thereby keeping enemies and chaos from coming into the temple.

The tops of the columns in this temple, re-created by a modern artist, look like the marsh plants found in the watery Nu.

Temples were frequently built on an east-west axis, the line of the sun's daily path. Near sunrise and sunset, a person would see the sun framed between the pylons. One pylon was said to represent Isis (mother of the young sun of the horizon, Horus), while the other represented her sister Nephthys. The Karnak temple complex also had buildings and avenues constructed on a north-south axis, echoing the path of the Nile River.

Within the temple precincts, the symbolism recalled the beginnings of life—the watery Nu and the marshy land that first appeared when the waters receded. The columns of the hypostyle hall were all made to look like marsh plants, with their capitals, or tops, in the shape of papyrus and lotus buds and flowers. The lower portions of the hall's walls were often decorated with more marsh plants. Higher on these walls, the art showed the king making offerings to the god. Above, the ceiling was painted to represent the sky.

Many temples had some kind of representation of the primeval mound where creation began. This might be an actual mound of earth, a mini pyramid or some kind of model or, as in the temple of Re-Atum at Heliopolis, a sacred object called the *benben* stone. In many temples, the inner sanctuary itself symbolized the primeval mound. Obelisks, too, might have represented the mound or *benben*—this is the opinion of some scholars, while others see obelisks as symbols of the sun's rays. What is clear, though, is that Egyptian temples were designed to celebrate creation and the power of the sun.

the main local god. When the New Kingdom pharaohs made Amen the country's chief god, they showed their devotion—and their own wealth and power—by adding to his temple on an ever grander scale.

By the end of the New Kingdom, Karnak had three separate walled enclosures: the precinct of Amen, the precinct of Mut, and the precinct of Montu. Amen's enclosure was in the center, linked to Mut's in the south by an avenue lined with ram-headed sphinxes. (The ram was one of Amen's sacred animals.) Within the precinct of Amen alone were nine pylons; about a dozen obelisks; an artificial lake; a temple of Ptah and one of Khonsu; a memorial temple to Pharaoh Thutmose III; various chapels, shrines, and other buildings; and several courtyards and halls. All of this was, of course, in addition to the sanctuary of Amen. And then there was the Great Hypostyle Hall, one of the masterpieces of ancient Egyptian architecture. Its 12 central columns rose to about 67 feet, flanked by 122 columns about 42 feet high and as much as 27.5 feet around. Karnak was a wonder even to the people who built it and worked in it. Pharaoh Amenhotep III described the entryway as "a very great portal . . . wrought with gold throughout. . . . Its floor is adorned with silver, towers are over against it. Stelae of lapis lazuli are set up, one on each side. Its pylons reach heaven like the four pillars of heaven, its flagstaffs shine more than the heavens, wrought with electrum."

The great temple complex is in ruins now, though still magnificent. But just imagine its grandeur during the New Kingdom, when the sandstone walls glowed in the sunlight. Sculptures, pillars, and reliefs were painted in vivid colors. Obelisks were tipped with glimmering gold leaf. Doors were made of imported cedarwood, often plated with copper or gold. The pillared halls, with their roofs intact, were cool and shadowy, hinting at the mysterious presence of the god in his inner sanctuary. Statues were everywhere. The scent of incense and lotus blossoms was in the air, and the music of hymns and harps and rattles could be heard. People moved about on the god's business—priests, priestesses, musicians, dancers, and servants, as well as artisans and workers employed to add even more beauty and splendor to the holy precincts.

SACRED ANIMALS

Many temples had animal residents contributing to the sacred precincts' activities, sounds, and smells. For example, the temple of Bast was home to hundreds (if not thousands) of cats and kittens, and Thoth's temples housed large numbers of the ibises and baboons sacred to him. Sacred animals became an even more important feature of religion later in Egyptian history. Throughout the centuries, though, the most celebrated of all these animals was probably the Apis bull.

The Apis bull carries a dead person into the afterlife. This painting was part of the decoration of a 3,500-year-old mummy case.

The Apis bull was associated with the god Ptah and lived in a sacred enclosure just south of Ptah's great temple in Memphis. There could be only one Apis at a time. When one of these bulls died, the priests of Ptah carried out a nationwide search for his successor. They would recognize him by his special markings: a white triangular blaze on his forehead and white spots on his back and neck. When a suitable calf was found, the priests (after rewarding the original owner) took both him and his mother back to Memphis. Both received the best care and treatment throughout their lives. When they died, their bodies were mummified and given honorable burials in special tombs.

Queen Nefertari offers pots of wine to the gods in this image from her beautifully painted tomb in the Valley of the Queens.

HOUSES OF ETERNITY

Just as the gods had their mansions, so too the dead required houses—especially dead kings. Most New Kingdom pharaohs were buried in the Great Place, or Valley of the Kings, on the west bank of the Nile, across the river from Thebes. Some queens, royal children, and favored courtiers were buried there as well. During the Nineteenth Dynasty, another cemetery, known today as the Valley of the Queens, was founded nearby especially for relatives of the pharaoh. More tombs of nobles and officials were also built in the area around Thebes, although many were buried near their own hometowns or in the north in the vicinity of the pyramids.

Some New Kingdom tombs were built of stone aboveground, often made to look like miniature temples. The more important tombs of this period, though—especially the royal ones—were rock-cut, dug into the desert cliffs. Constructing these tombs was a long and arduous process. The builders had only simple mechanical aids, such as levers, and their tools were made of copper, bronze, wood, and stone. The sole light underground came from oil lamps or, closer to the surface, mirrors arranged to reflect sunlight into the tomb.

Work on a king's tomb usually began shortly after he came to the throne—if not at some point while he was still crown prince. Even so, most tombs were not finished before they were needed. Once a king died, it took about seventy days for his mummy to be prepared, and that was all the time the workers had to finish the building, decorating, and furnishing of his final resting place.

There was no standard design for these tombs, but generally they had a long entrance passageway with steps and ramps leading downward into the rock. This symbolized the sun's nighttime journey in the underworld, which was often illustrated on the passage walls. Then came a squarish room, sometimes called the Hall of Waiting. From here a short corridor might lead into a pillared hall. There could be other anterooms, as well as storerooms for various grave goods. At the very back of the tomb was the burial chamber itself. In its center stood the huge stone sarcophagus that contained the mummy inside its nest of coffins.

It was an Egyptian belief that a person's body had to be preserved so that he or she could enjoy the afterlife. This was the reason for mummies, and for tombs to house and protect them. Tombs were also stocked with clothing, furniture, makeup kits, jewelry, games, weapons, food, and all sorts of other things for the deceased's use and enjoyment. In addition, there might be symbolic or ceremonial objects, such as models of the boat that the sun

The approach to the tomb of Ramses IX in the Valley of the Kings. The entrance was originally well hidden (in an attempt to protect the tomb from robbers) but is now accessible to tourists.

sailed through the underworld. In royal burials from the Eighteenth Dynasty, there was often a wooden tray shaped like the god Osiris, which would have been filled with dirt and planted with grain seeds to symbolize life continuing after death. And just in case life after death was not all rest and relaxation, many tombs included statuettes of the mummified tomb owner, which could be called on to do any work required. Such a figure was called a *shabti* (or *ushebti*), and it was empowered by the words written on it:

> O shabti, allotted to me, if I be summoned or if I be detailed to do any work which has to be done in the God's Domain . . . , you shall detail yourself for me on every occasion of making arable the fields, of flooding the banks, or of conveying sand from east to west; "Here am I," you shall say.

The tomb walls were painted, or carved and painted, with scenes of the afterlife. In nonroyal tombs, there might also be paintings showing everyday life. Sometimes the ceiling of the burial chamber was decorated to look like the night sky, symbolizing the goddess Nut's body arching protectively over the sarcophagus. Nearly all of the images in the tomb, not just those of the gods, were there for symbolic or religious reasons. For example, scenes from the dead person's life demonstrated his or her worthiness to enjoy the blessings of immortality. The deceased was nearly always portrayed in an idealized fashion, fit and vigorous and in the prime of life—because that, of course, was how he or she would want to be in the afterlife.

Hieroglyphic texts were also an important part of the tomb's wall decoration. Some of these functioned mainly as "captions" for the painted images. Others were selections from various books of the afterlife, which contained hymns to the gods, instructions for passing through the different parts of the underworld, and similar materials. In nonroyal tombs, these texts were painted not on the walls but inside the coffin, or the actual papyrus books were included in the burial. In whatever form, the words had power. Together with the images and grave goods, they created a symbolic version of the afterlife, which the power of the gods could turn into true immortality for the deceased.

THREE

PRIESTS

There were hundreds of temples in Egypt, and the chief priest of every one of them, and of every god, was the pharaoh himself. Indeed, the pharaoh was often thought of as being a god on Earth, or at least semidivine. And because he was partly human and partly divine, he was the ideal person to connect the people of Egypt to their gods.

Of course, the king could not be in every temple, performing every ritual, every day. The Egyptians dealt with this in two ways. First, each temple had at least one image of him making offerings to the temple's deity. To the Egyptians, artwork of this type had a magical power to make the things it depicted real, at least in the sight of the gods. Second, all other priests were regarded as standing in for the king, making the offerings on his behalf and under his direction.

Opposite:
The pharaoh was chief priest of all the gods. Here Ramses III pours a libation (a liquid offering) and presents smoking incense in a ceremony depicted in his tomb.

The goddess Mut, wife of Amen. This divine couple protected kings and queens, and the pharaoh played the lead role in an annual festival in which the statues of Amen and Mut traveled from one temple to another.

SERVING THE GOD

Ancient Egyptian priests were not clergy in the sense that most of us are familiar with. They did not lead worship services, preach sermons, explain religious teachings, or counsel people. Instead, their job was to serve the deity of the temple that employed them, and through this service to uphold *maat*, the divine order, throughout Egypt.

Each deity had a high priest, known as the First Prophet or First Servant of the God. Some of these had additional titles. The chief priest of Ptah, for example, was called "Lord of the Master Craftsmen"; the First Prophet of Re at Heliopolis was "Greatest of Seers." Immediately beneath these temple leaders were a few other priests holding the rank of prophet. It was only the members of this highest level of the priesthood (and the pharaoh), along with those who assisted them in specific ceremonies, who were allowed to enter the god's sanctuary and see him face-to-face.

Every morning one of the prophets performed the all-important daily ritual. With the proper prayers, he opened the sanctuary and lit a torch, symbolizing the sunrise. Then he recited more prayers as he purified the air with incense. He removed the clothes that had been draped on the statue the day before and washed it thoroughly, also purifying it with more incense. After the priest anointed the statue with perfumed oil, dressed it in fresh linen, and adorned it with jewelry, he laid offerings before it, including food and drink. Now he called to the spirit of the god, "Come to your body! Come to . . . your servant who does not forget his part in your feasts! Bring your power, your magic and your honour to this bread which is warm, to this beer which is warm, to this roast which is warm."

The god was given time to enjoy the spiritual essence of the offerings. Then they were removed and distributed among the temple priests, according to rank, or put into the temple warehouses. Meanwhile, the statue was cleansed and purified again, and clean sand was sprinkled over the sanctuary floor. When the priest left, he backed out, bowing and sweeping away his footsteps with a broom. At the end of the day, he closed the sanctuary doors and "locked" them with a mud seal so that the god could rest undisturbed through the night.

The prophets, or Servants of the God, were full-time clergymen. The majority of priests, though, worked only one month out of every four at the temple, and held other jobs the rest of the time. A few days before a man's month of service started, he began purifying himself by burning incense and chewing natron (a salt, which was also used as a soap substitute and for preparing mummies). Prior to leaving his home for the temple, he bathed thoroughly, trimmed his fingernails and toenails, and shaved all the hair from his head, face, and body. He was required to remain ritually pure throughout the time he served, which meant staying clean and hairless, not sleeping with his wife, and observing whatever other prohibitions his temple might impose—for example, not eating any fish for the month. For this reason, these ordinary priests were called "pure ones." They were responsible for purifying anything that was brought into the temple and keeping ceremonial objects in a proper state of cleanliness.

Another group of men who served in some temples were known as lector priests. During ceremonies they read or chanted the sacred writings carved on the temple's walls or written in its books. Lector priests were often scribes and scholars and might work in the part

A PRIEST LOOKS BACK ON HIS LIFE

Upper-class Egyptians often had their autobiographies inscribed on their tomb walls—a great resource for modern people studying ancient Egypt. Here is some of the autobiography of Beknekhonsu, telling how he moved up through the ranks of the priesthood and describing some of his duties as First Prophet of Amen during the reign of Ramses II.

A scribe burns incense before food offerings to the god Osiris.

I was a truthful witness, profitable to his lord, extolling the instructions of the god, proceeding upon his way, performing the excellent ceremonies in the midst of his temple. I was chief overseer of works in the house of Amon [Amen], satisfying the excellent heart of his lord. . . . I will inform you of my character while I was upon earth, in every office I administered, since my birth.

I passed four years in extreme childhood.
I passed twelve years as a youth. . . .
I acted as priest of Amon, during four years.
I acted as divine father of Amon, during twelve years.
I acted as third prophet of Amon, during fifteen years.
I acted as second prophet of Amon, during twelve years.
He favoured me, he distinguished me, because of my rare merit. He appointed me to be High Priest of Amon during twenty-seven years.

I was a good father to my serf-laborers, training their classes, giving my hand [to] him who was in trouble, preserving alive him who was in misfortune. . . .

I performed the excellent duties in the house of Amon. . . . I made for him a temple (called) Ramses-Meriamon-Hearer-of-Petitions, at the upper portal of the house of Amon. I erected obelisks therein, of granite, whose beauty approached heaven. A wall was before it of stone over against Thebes; it was flooded, and the gardens were planted with trees. I made very great double doors of electrum; their beauty met the heavens.

of the temple called the House of Life, where records and religious texts were produced and stored.

There were other kinds of priests, too. *Sem* priests officiated at funerals and were not necessarily affiliated with temples. Often, a dead person's oldest son acted as *sem* priest. *Ka* priests, too, could be family members. They were in charge of offerings to the dead. When the deceased was a pharaoh, however, the offerings were made at a temple dedicated to him, called a mortuary or memorial temple. Here there would be a large staff of priests, organized as in the temples of the great gods.

MEN OF POWER AND LEARNING

In addition to the honor and satisfaction of serving the deities, even a part-time career in the priesthood gave a man a number of worldly benefits. Priests were exempt from paying many taxes. They also shared in the offerings brought to their temples and in the produce raised on temple lands. In the higher ranks, priests could become men of great wealth and influence. The First Prophet of Amen was one of the most powerful men in New Kingdom Egypt. In fact, in the period after the New Kingdom, Amen's high priests were the virtual rulers of southern Egypt for several generations.

Like an earthly king or noble, a god might own a great deal of property besides his mansion. For example, records from the Twentieth Dynasty tell us that the god Amen's possessions included "86,486 serfs, 421,362 head of cattle, 433 gardens and orchards, 691,334 acres of land, 83 ships, 46 workshops, 65 cities and towns, plus gold, silver, incense and other valuables in unmeasured amounts." Naturally, somebody had to look after all this wealth— and that was the job of most temple personnel. By the midpoint of the New Kingdom, roughly one-third of Egypt's farmland was owned by the temples. This gave them, and their priests, a very

A scribe sits in his typical working pose: cross-legged, with a papyrus scroll unrolled in his lap.

powerful role in the Egyptian economy.

There was another kind of power that centered on Egypt's temples, and that was the power of knowledge. Most Egyptians could neither read nor write, but in the major temples there were educated priests and large numbers of scribes (specialists in reading and writing). The House of Life was a kind of library and a center of learning, where boys of the upper classes came to study so that they could become scribes or priests or government officials. The common people could come to the outer, public parts of the temple to hire scribes to write prayers, letters, and legal documents for them.

Medicine was another branch of learning that flourished in the temples. The House of Life trained doctors as well as scribes, and ordinary people could seek medical treatment from physician-priests. The ancient Egyptians possessed the most advanced medical knowledge in the ancient world. They realized that the pulse was the "voice of the heart," and they understood the functions of many bodily organs. They knew a great deal about the healing properties of various plants and other substances. Still, there was much they could not know or do without modern methods of diagnosis and treatment. For this reason, many treatments were (from a modern viewpoint) more magical than medical in nature.

In fact, to the ancient Egyptians, magic was simply another area of advanced learning, which applied specialized knowledge for both religious and practical purposes. It was one of the gifts the gods gave humans to help them in life as well as death. Several deities were especially concerned with magic, such as Heka (the divine personification of magic), Thoth, and Isis, whom legend called "a woman skilled in words." Words were very powerful to the ancient Egyptians—the term that the Egyptians most often used for hieroglyphic writing literally meant "the god's words"—and they were among a magician's primary tools.

People in all walks of life used magic in various forms. Much magical activity, however, centered on the temples (lector priests were widely known as magicians), especially when writing was involved. For example, some of the work that people came to hire scribes for involved writing out spells or inscribing amulets with magical formulas. Some spells, though, were secrets of the temple, such as one for creating an amulet to ward off crocodiles; it begins, "The first spell of all water-songs, about which the magician has said, 'Do not reveal it to the common man! It is a secret of the House of Life.'"

As a god of words and wisdom, ibis-headed Thoth concerned himself with all kinds of knowledge, including magic.

FOUR

WOMEN AND RELIGION

In some ancient societies, women had few (if any) opportunities to publicly or officially participate in religion. In this, as in other ways, Egyptian women were freer than many others. The religious roles available to women did change over time, however. In earlier periods they had been able to hold high-ranking priesthoods in some temples, especially those of Hathor, the goddess of women. During the New Kingdom, these positions of power were open only to men. Nevertheless, women could still take part in important ways in the worship of the deities in their temples.

DIVINE MUSIC

Women's major role in Egyptian temples was to participate in ceremonies and provide entertainment for the gods as singers, musicians, and dancers. They performed hymns that affirmed the

Opposite:
The goddess Hathor in human form, adorned with cobras. The snakes represented the Eye of Re and also symbolized royalty, divine authority, and protection.

A priestess holds a bundle of papyrus flowers and plays a sistrum decorated with the face of Hathor.

upholding of *maat:* the deity was great and generous, and people in turn honored the deity with their praise and offerings. There was balance between the divine and humanity, and all was well in the world.

"Holy music for Hathor, music a million times, because you love music, million times music, to your soul, wherever you are," went a song to the goddess who was most associated with music. One instrument that women often played in temple rituals, the sistrum, was especially sacred to Hathor—her image might even be incorporated into its design. It was shaped much like an ankh (the hiero-glyph that meant "life"), a T with a loop above the crossbar. Into the sistrum's loop were set three or four thin metal rods, often threaded with metal disks. When a musician shook the sistrum, the metal pieces jingled together.

Rhythm instruments seem to have been especially important in temple music. In her other hand, a sistrum player might hold a heavy beaded necklace, which rattled when she shook it. Another musical instrument that women frequently played in religious ceremonies was the tambourine—the goddesses Isis and Hathor in particular seemed to favor it. Hand-clapping, too, added rhythmic accompaniment to sacred songs. And sometimes musicians played clappers made of wood or ivory, probably producing a sound resembling that of castanets.

To make sure that everyone played their best, temple "orchestras" (which might include men as well as women) had regular practice sessions. The musicians could be called on to play "every day at any hour" the god wished. In some temples, probably, there were specific ceremonies for each hour of the day. Many of these would have been enhanced by singing and dancing.

Upper-class women often served in temples as singers with the special title "chantress of the god." As the wives and daughters of priests and government officials, these women were already highly respected. Their temple activities—singing, chanting, and playing the sistrum—brought them and their families further honor, and probably a share in the temple's wealth, too.

The long-necked lute was one of the instruments commonly played by women, both in temple orchestras and in ensembles that entertained at banquets and other festivities.

THE QUEEN AND THE GODS

While the pharaoh was chief priest of all the gods, his wife was not quite so highly exalted. Still, she had important religious roles. Just as the king could represent various gods, the queen was associated with goddesses, especially Isis, Hathor, and Mut. The connection was shown in various ways. For example, a queen might wear the special headdress of one of the goddesses or be portrayed in the typical pose of a particular goddess. Queen Tiy, the wife of Amenhotep III, was compared to Maat: "The Principal Wife of the King, beloved of him, Tiy, may she live. It is like Maat following Re that she is in the following of Your Majesty." Indeed, the marriage between a king

The pharaoh Hatshepsut had herself portrayed as a sphinx in this colossal stone statue.

and queen was a symbol of the balance between male and female that was an important part of *maat*.

Some queens early in the New Kingdom held the title God's Wife of Amen. In this role they performed various public religious duties, such as taking part in processions with Amen's priests. Hatshepsut, as the wife of Thutmose II, was the last New Kingdom queen to bear this title. After her husband's death, she took on an even loftier role: she became pharaoh herself. This, she said on an obelisk she commissioned for the Karnak temple, was the will of the gods:

Amen, Lord of Thrones of the Two Lands caused me to rule the Red Land and the Black Land as a reward. No one rebels against me in all my lands . . . I am his daughter in very truth, she who serves him and knows what he ordains. My reward from my father is life-stability-dominion on the Horus-throne of all the living, like Re forever.

Hatshepsut showed her devotion to her divine father Amen by making a number of additions to Karnak. She also supported the construction of temples and shrines to Hathor. Her own splendid mortuary temple near the Valley of the Kings included chapels dedicated to Amen, Hathor, and Anubis, as well as to herself and her father, Thutmose I. Her monuments frequently show her engaging in traditional kingly activities, many of a religious nature.

A few generations later, another famous queen, Nefertiti, also took on some of the king's religious functions. Reliefs from one of her husband Akhenaten's temples to the sun god Aten portray her as though she is making offerings to the god—that is, doing the king's job. Other evidence shows that Nefertiti may well have been a full co-ruler of Egypt with the king. Nearly all queens afterward, however, kept to the expected queenly role. It was a praiseworthy role, though, as shown by this loving description of Queen Nefertari, wife of Ramses II, worshipping Amen:

See her, her hands here shaking the sistra
to bring pleasure to God, her father Amun.
How lovely she moves,
her hair bound with fillets,
Songstress with perfect features,
a beauty in double-plumed headdress.

FIVE

FROM BIRTH TO DEATH AND BEYOND

When the ancient Egyptians looked at their world, they saw opposites alternating and balancing each other—day and night, farmland and desert, life and death. They saw cycles, too: the changing seasons, the daily round of the sun. Awareness of all these processes wove into their beliefs and into the way they lived their lives. At the same time, the way they lived their lives influenced what they believed and the way they looked at nature's balance and cycles. Life and religion mirrored each other, and were part of each other.

The journey of the sun played a central role in Egyptian beliefs, and it was something everyone could observe and feel the effects of. Since the most common form of transportation was by boat on the Nile, people thought of the sun as sailing a boat across the sky during the day, and sailing another boat through the underworld at night. At the same time, it was easy to picture the sun having a life

Opposite:
A woman mourns before the mummy of a loved one, supported by a priest.

The sun god Re, accompanied by other deities, begins his daily journey in the solar boat.

like that of humans. The sun god was born in the morning, reached the full strength of adulthood at noon, grew old with the evening, and at night went to the underworld. There he returned to the womb of the sky goddess Nut and waited to be reborn the next day.

CHILDBIRTH AND CHILDREN

It pleased the Egyptians to know that their deities shared in many aspects of human life. Family was extremely important to the Egyptians, and it was to the gods as well—many, if not most, deities were grouped together in triads as mother, father, and child. And although divine parents did not face the same troubles as their human counterparts, they understood them.

The Egyptians often turned to the gods for help when it came to pregnancy, birth, and children. Women who wanted to become pregnant might pray and offer figurines to Hathor or to the blessed dead. One woman, for example, left a statuette of a mother and child at a tomb; inscribed on the image was the prayer, "May a birth be granted to your daughter Seh." Would-be fathers also made offerings. The scribe Ramose oversaw construction of a temple to Hathor in his village and left the goddess a stone on which he had carved a plea for children to carry on his family and memory after death: "Hathor, remember the man at his burial. Grant a duration in your house as a reward for the scribe Ramose, O Golden One—let me receive a compensation of your house [a child] as one rewarded."

Once a woman became pregnant, she had even more need of divine aid. Many things could go wrong during pregnancy, and childbirth was extremely dangerous—many mothers and babies died during it or soon after. A goddess who took the form of a pregnant hippopotamus, Taweret ("The Great One"), was one of the helpers pregnant women turned to. They wore amulets of her image and kept statuettes or paintings of her in their houses. She was often shown carrying a knife and making a hideous face to frighten away evil spirits. She might also be portrayed holding the hieroglyph for "protection" or for "life."

When a baby was born, the mother immediately named it. Egyptian personal names often incorporated names of the gods, as we can see in the case of many pharaohs— Thutmose (Thoth), Amenhotep (Amen), Horemheb (Horus), Seti (Seth), Ramses (Re), Merenptah (Ptah)—as well as queens and princesses, for example Meretaten (Aten), Mutnodjmet (Mut), Isetnofret (Isis), and Maatnefrure (Maat). These sorts of names were not just for royalty, either; names such as Merybast ("beloved of Bast") appear often among commoners. So, sometimes, do very long names, like Pediamennebnesttawy—

Taweret, "The Great One," rests her strong paw on the hieroglyph for "protection."

which meant "Gift of Amen who is Lord of the Thrones of the Two Lands."

Although safely born and safely named, a baby was still not out of danger. Young children were highly vulnerable to illness, and many did not live more than a few years. For protection, anxious parents gave their children amulets, worn on necklaces and braided into their hair. Many amulets were in the shape of deities, hiero-glyphs, or symbols. Another type of amulet was a piece of papyrus with a spell written on it, rolled up tight and fitted inside a bead that the child could wear. To activate the spell, the parents probably had to speak it aloud. To repel a spirit that caused sudden illness, the spell might be like this one: "Perish, you who come in from the dark. You who creep in with your nose reversed and your face turned back, and who forgets what he came for. Did you come to kiss this child? I will not allow you to kiss him."

Childhood, with all its perils, did not last long; people began to take on adult roles as young teenagers. It was usual for children to follow in their parents' footsteps, so the sons and daughters of priests and priestesses often joined the priesthood, too. The highest ranks of priests, though, generally seem to have been appointed by the pharaoh. If he had many sons, he might give priestly offices to some of them. Ramses II's son Khaemwaset, for example, became the chief priest of Ptah—and was so active and devoted in his office that his scholarship and achievements were still renowned a thousand years later.

WORKING WITH THE GODS

As adults, even people who did not become priests or priestesses often felt the presence of the gods in their working lives. Many were employed by the temples. Some worked "on site" as servants, crafts-people, or builders. Others labored on estates owned by the great temples, farming the gods' lands and herding their cattle. The men who worked to build the tombs in the Valley of the Kings seem to have been especially conscious of the gods' influence as they worked. They left behind graffiti and many sketches on limestone flakes that expressed their devotion to various deities in both words and pictures.

Many professions had special relationships with particular gods. People in these jobs would make a point of honoring their patron deities and would pray to them for success in their labors. For instance, every morning before a scribe began his work, he sprinkled a bit of water on the ground in honor of Thoth, the patron of scribes. Some other patron deities were Ptah, for craftspeople; Anubis, for embalmers; and Imhotep, for doctors. Some dancers and musicians honored their special god, Bes, by tattooing themselves with his image.

Although some women worked as musicians and dancers, most worked in the home. Here, too, Bes might watch over them. Pictures and statues of Bes appeared in many homes of the common people. He was one of the guardians of the household, probably because his grotesque face was believed to frighten away demons and other harmful forces.

When doing outdoor work, women and men alike had to keep alert to avoid harmful animals, especially crocodiles (when near water), scorpions, and poisonous snakes. Many Egyptians during

The popular god Bes was honored throughout Egypt and in many territories ruled by the Egyptians. This ivory carving of Bes was found in Megiddo, in what is now Israel.

the New Kingdom worshipped a god named Shed (or Hor-Shed), whose name meant "rescuer" or "savior." He was pictured as a soldier who trod on crocodiles, snakes, and scorpions. It seems that only ordinary working people appealed to him for help since, so far as we know, he had no official priesthood or temples.

In a funeral procession, two men mourn the death of their father.

DEATH AND THE AFTERLIFE

Many people think that the ancient Egyptians were obsessed with death. After all, look at the elaborate care they took with their burials. But when we really examine those burials—especially the paintings on tomb walls—we get a different picture, one that shows us a people who passionately loved life. They loved it so much that they simply wanted it to go on and on—only without the troubles of life on Earth.

To get to the joys of the afterlife, however, was no simple matter. People of means began planning for death many years before they reached old age, ordering and overseeing the preparation of a suitable tomb. When death came, the family entered a period of mourning while the deceased was mummified. This lengthy process involved removing and preserving the internal organs, drying the body, then wrapping it in linen bands. Within the linen were placed many amulets, intended to help the dead person on the journey into eternity. The most important of these amulets was in the shape of a scarab, placed over the heart. On it was written, "O my heart which I had from my mother, . . . do not rise up against me as a witness in the presence of the Lord of Things."

When the mummy was ready, the funeral was held. In a procession to the tomb, the family was accompanied by priests who played the roles of Anubis and other gods, two women who represented Isis and Nephthys, hired women mourners, and servants carrying grave goods and offerings. At the tomb the deceased's oldest son, or a priest acting for him, performed the ceremony of "opening the mouth," touching the mummy's mouth, eyes, and ears with a special tool and reciting the words that would allow the deceased the use of his or her senses in the afterlife. Then, after a funeral feast, the mummy would be laid in its final resting place and the tomb would be sealed.

The dead person was now referred to as Osiris (or "the Osiris _____," with the blank being filled in with the deceased's name). In the underworld, the Osiris undertook a difficult, dangerous journey, like that the sun endured every night. Eventually he or she reached the Hall of Judgment and came before the throne of the great god Osiris, lord of the dead. Here, as the Ennead watched and the scribe-god Thoth stood by to take note of the result, the Osiris's heart was weighed against the feather of Maat, the symbl of truth. If the heart balanced with the feather, Thoth would declare to the Ennead, "I have judged the heart of the deceased, and his soul stands as a witness for him. His deeds are righteous in the great balance, and no sin has been found in him." Then the Ennead would reply:

> The vindicated Osiris [name] is straightforward, he
> has no sin. . . . Ammit [the monster who devoured

This scarab amulet from the tomb of Tutankhamen depicts the god Khepri pushing the rising sun up over the horizon, a powerful symbol of rebirth. The amulet is made of gold and semiprecious stones, including lapis lazuli for the scarab's body and carnelian for the sun.

ISIS AND OSIRIS

Osiris was one of Egypt's most beloved gods, and his story gave hope and spiritual comfort to people in all walks of life. He had been the first king of Egypt—indeed, the first king on Earth—and had taught humans the art of agriculture. The land flourished under him: "for his sake green things grew, and the good earth would bring forth its riches." The people lived in peace and plenty, and he governed so well that all the gods praised and admired him. All but one: his brother Seth grew jealous and plotted against him. Seth succeeded in killing Osiris and scattered the pieces of his body throughout Egypt. But Osiris' sister-wife, Isis, did not accept his death and determined to reassemble his body:

> His sister served as shield and defender,
>> beat off the enemies,
> Ended unspeakable mischief by power of her spell,
>> golden-tongued goddess
>>> (her voice shall not fail),
> Skilled to command,
>> beneficent Isis,
>>> who rescued her brother.
> Who searched for him
>> and would not surrender to weariness,
> Wandered this earth bent with anguish,
>> restless until she had found him. . . .
> Performed the rites of his resurrection,
>> moored, married, made breathe her brother,
> Put life in the slackened limbs
>> of the good god whose heart had grown weary.

After bringing Osiris back to life, Isis gave birth to their son, Horus. When he was grown, he succeeded his father as king on Earth, and Osiris went to rule in the underworld. And as Isis had protected Osiris, so she helped the dead on their journey into eternal life: "May your arms be beside the Osiris," says a prayer to Isis carved on a queen's sarcophagus. "Make her face shine brightly and open her eyes."

unrighteous souls] shall not be permitted to have power over him. Let there be given to him the offerings which are issued in the presence of Osiris, and may a grant of land be established in the Field of Offerings as for the Followers of Horus.

Now at last the Osiris could dwell among the gods, travel with the sun in his ship, and enjoy the beautiful fields of the otherworld. And so, the just man received the gift of the afterlife.

These beliefs about death and the afterlife were preserved in the tombs and grave goods of upper-class Egyptians. The great majority of the people, however, were humble farmers and laborers, who could not afford mummies and tombs. Their funerals were not fancy—although certainly their families prayed and mourned for them—and they were most likely simply wrapped in a bit of linen and buried in plain graves beneath the desert sands. Still, we can assume that they, too, hoped for a happy hereafter in the presence of the gods.

With Thoth perched atop the scales in baboon form, the god Anubis weighs a dead man's heart against the feather of Maat. On the upper right the deceased's *ba*, an aspect of his soul shown as a human-headed bird, awaits the outcome.

SIX

HOLIDAYS AND EVERY DAY

Relating to the divine, living a moral life, preparing for an afterlife—these are the kinds of things that the word *religion* means to most modern people. As in many ancient cultures, however, the Egyptians had no concept of religion in this way; they did not even have a word for it. The things that we call religion didn't need their own name because they never seemed to be in a category of their own—they were too interwoven with every aspect of life to be separated out. Even a simple, businesslike letter matter-of-factly included the gods:

> The mayor Mentuhotpe greets the scribe Ahmose . . .
> in life, prosperity and health, and in the favour of
> Amon-Re, King of the Gods, of Atum, Lord of
> Heliopolis, Re-Horakhty, Thoth, Lord of god's words,
> Seshat (?), Lady of writing, and your noble god who

Opposite:
Gods and goddesses were a part of every aspect of life in ancient Egypt. Here Ptah is shown holding an ankh, the hieroglyph for "life."

loves you; may they give you favour, love and cleverness wherever you are [or in whatever you do]. Further: you should have installed the matting and beams of the store-rooms together with the back part of the house. . . . And you should instruct the builder, Amenmose, so that he does it just so, and hastens the building of the house. See to it!

THE DEVOTION OF THE PEOPLE

As we have seen, the great temples were mainly the domain of priests—ordinary Egyptians never entered the inner areas. The outer courts, though, were open to them, especially on festival days.

In the outer sections, too, or just outside the temple enclosure, there were often shrines that could be visited by anyone. Sometimes these were "ear shrines," decorated with images of the deity's ears as a sign that the god would hear his worshippers' prayers. Many New Kingdom prayers express confidence in the gods' willingness to respond to the concerns of humble people; for instance: "You are Amen, the Lord of the silent, who pays heed to the voice of the poor. When I call to you in my distress you come to rescue me."

Occasionally someone might feel that praying at an ear shrine was not enough. We know of at

One of many stelae found in an "ear shrine" at a temple in Memphis. In the center is a hieroglyphic inscription praising the god Ptah. This plaque was set up by a man named Mahwia, who clearly believed in Ptah's willingness to hear his prayers.

least one example of a man who went to a temple hoping to lay his problems directly before the god (embodied by the statue in the sanctuary). Unfortunately, he was not of the priestly rank that would allow him past the outer areas of the temple. So he waited around until a priest of appropriate rank came along, then wrote or dictated a letter to the god for the priest to deliver: "There was nobody having access to it [the sanctuary] to send in to you. But as I was waiting, I met Hori . . . and he said to me, 'I have access'. So I am sending him to you."

In Egypt's villages, it seems likely that people rarely had much to do with the great temples. They had their own, much smaller, temples and shrines, where they worshipped their local deities. For example, people in the tomb workers' village outside Thebes were especially devoted to the deified Amenhotep I, said to have been the founder of their community. They filled his little temple with offerings, stelae, and statues, and held several festivals every year in honor of him and his mother, Ahmose-Nefertari.

An ancient model of the garden courtyard of a wealthy Egyptian's home. This would have been a perfect location for a family chapel.

Egyptians in many places and of many ranks also worshipped at household shrines. Often this was just a cupboard or niche in the wall of the house's main room, although a wealthier family might build a chapel in the garden. Sometimes the deities honored at village and household shrines were popular national gods and goddesses, such as Osiris and Hathor. We have seen, too, how the common people often looked to Shed, Taweret, and Bes. Another deity important to the ordinary Egyptian was the cobra goddess Renenutet, whose name meant "Provider of Nourishment." She was a goddess of breastfeeding and the harvest, when grain was offered to her, and her image was painted on the walls of many village chapels.

Finally, every family had their beloved dead to care for. The recently deceased were probably still thought of as part of the family. They were honored at the household shrine, and their graves were visited often. If the deceased had been well-off enough to be buried in a tomb, outside it would be a chapel where family members could make offerings, commune with the spirit of their loved one, and feast together on special holidays. Some people even left letters for the dead asking for various kinds of help; one person wrote to an ancestor, "Become an *akh* ["able spirit"] for me before my eyes so that I can see you in a dream fighting on my behalf. I will then deposit offerings for you."

SPECIAL PLACES, SPECIAL DAYS

Occasionally people traveled from home to visit a sacred site. Most pilgrims would probably stick with sites in their own local region. A major temple complex or monument, however, might attract people from some distance. That is the impression we get with regard to the Great Sphinx of Giza; a stela between its front paws tells us that "Memphis and every city on its two sides came to him, their arms in adoration to his face, bearing great offerings to his *ka*."

Many people made pilgrimages to Abydos, the traditional burial place of Osiris, where they set up memorial stelae to their

beloved dead and left messages to the god written on pieces of broken pots. The pilgrims often timed their visit to Abydos so that they would be there for the great eight-day festival of Osiris. On the first day, a procession of priests and priestesses, acting the parts of the characters in the Osiris story, escorted the god's statue to its tomb. After the "burial," there were three days and nights of mourning, led by the priestesses playing Isis and Nephthys. Then came a reenactment of Seth's trial before the deities for the murder of Osiris. On the next day, the festival participants staged a mock battle between the followers of the two gods. Osiris's side was victorious, of course, and the god was brought triumphantly out of his tomb. The priests ended the festival by

The Great Sphinx of Giza awed ancient pilgrims at least as much as it does modern travelers. At the time of the New Kingdom, the Sphinx was already more than a thousand years old.

setting up a sacred pillar, the *djed,* that represented Osiris's backbone; its raising symbolized his resurrection, and therefore that of all the blessed dead.

Thebes was also the scene of great festivals. The two most important, attended by the pharaoh himself, were Opet and the Feast of the Valley. Opet was a twenty-day celebration that centered on Amen's sacred image leaving the Karnak temple to visit the Luxor temple, a little over a mile to the south. The god's statue was placed within a golden shrine, veiled in linen, which traveled up the Nile on a gilded cedarwood barge. It was followed by barges carrying the statues of Mut and Khonsu, Amen's family. During the journey, the king and the chief priest burned incense to the

An amulet in the shape of a *djed* pillar, a symbol of stability and resurrection

god and offered him food. Cheering crowds watched the waterborne procession from the riverbank as musicians and dancers performed in honor of the holy family. On arrival at Luxor, the gods received a splendid welcome. Then, within the temple's inner sanctuary, the pharaoh made more offerings to Amen and took part in ceremonies to renew his spirit and his links with the gods. There was much pageantry during Amen's stay in Luxor, and his eventual return to Karnak was as magnificent as his outward journey had been.

On the Feast of the Valley, Amen again left his inner sanctuary and went aboard his barge. This time he crossed the Nile to the west bank, and there his shrine was placed in a boat-shaped litter, to be carried on the shoulders of his priests. Again there was a great procession, with music and dancing and incense and crowds of onlookers and worshippers. There were many stops along the processional route so that the god could receive offerings of flowers at small shrines, his bearers could rest, and people could come forward to ask him a question or simply get a closer look at his shrine. During the course of this festival, Amen was taken to visit each of the royal mortuary temples. He was accompanied by the pharaoh, and so the king of the gods, the dead kings who now resided with the gods, and the living king were joined together in harmony.

Holidays like these were the ordinary person's only opportunities to approach the sacred images of the great national deities such as Amen. To many Egyptians, though, probably

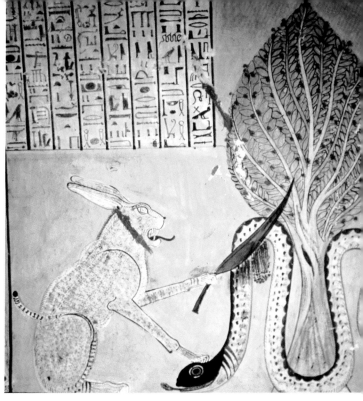

their own town and village festivals were even more important. They gave people the chance to honor and commune with their local gods and to relax, feast, and celebrate with their community. As a festival hymn began, "Rejoicing in heaven / joy on earth!"— the celebration of festivals large and small reminded everyone of their connections to the divine.

Re in the form of the Great Cat defeats the underworld serpent Apep, preventing him from devouring the sun during the night. To the ancient Egyptians, every dawn was a celebration of Re's victory.

ORACLES AND DREAMS

One of the ways that the common people sought the help of the gods was through an oracle. This was usually done when the local god's statue was carried in procession on a holiday. Then anyone could step out of the crowd and ask the god a yes/no question; the god would cause the priests carrying his statue to move forward (for yes) or backward (no) in response. For a "multiple choice" question, the person could write (or draw a symbol for) each option on a separate limestone flake and lay them all out in the god's path, then watch to see if the god tended to move toward one more than the others. When the oracle wasn't available, or its meaning was

HOW HUMANITY WAS SAVED FROM DESTRUCTION

This is a story that was probably told during the annual Festival of Hathor—and it explains why drinking beer was an important part of the celebration. (Beer was also the normal, everyday drink of the ancient Egyptians. It was much thicker, more nutritious, and less alcoholic than modern beer.)

Re, king of gods and humans, discovered that humankind was plotting against him. He summoned a council of deities, who gave him encouraging advice: "Sit on your throne with confidence, for great would be the fear of you if your Eye were turned against those who are plotting against you." Indeed, people were already fleeing into the desert out of fear of Re's anger. The divine council urged him, "Cause your Eye to go that it may catch for you those who scheme evilly. . . . Let it go down as Hathor."

So Hathor went down into the desert, and there she began to devour humankind. Her ferocity awakened, she found she relished the task: "I have prevailed over humankind, and it is pleasant in my heart." Re had wanted her to simply teach a lesson to those plotting against him, but Hathor was now determined to destroy all the people of Egypt.

Quickly Re summoned servants to crush barley, and others to crush red ochre. The barley was made into beer—seven thousand jars of it—to which the ochre was added, dying it red. Re inspected the beer and said, "How good it is! I shall protect humankind with it." He ordered his servants to take it to the place where Hathor was going to slay the last remaining humans. When they poured out the red beer, it looked like blood, which soon attracted the fierce goddess.

Hathor was pleased. "She drank, and it was good in her heart." She became so drunk on the red beer that she forgot all about slaughtering humankind, and never thought of it again. From then on, Re called Hathor the Beautiful One, and decreed that people should always brew beer in her honor.

Above: Hathor as a beautiful young woman crowned with cow horns, cobra, and solar disk

unclear, some villagers were known to consult with "the wise woman," probably an older woman with a reputation as a seer.

The gods could also communicate with people through dreams. The most famous example of this is a dream that a young prince had in which the Great Sphinx appeared to him as a form of the sun god, promising him, "I shall give you the kingship." In return, the prince was asked to clear away the sand that had buried much of the Sphinx; he did so, and went on to become Pharaoh Thutmose IV. Dreams could come to anyone, however, not just future pharaohs. And if the meaning of a nighttime vision was unclear to a person, he or she could go to a priest for understanding. In a puzzling case, a priest might refer to a book of standard dream interpretations, in which he would read information such as the following:

> If a man sees himself in a dream slaughtering an ox with
>   his [own] hand, good: it means killing his adversary.
> Eating crocodile [flesh], good: it means acting as an official
>   among his people.
> Submerging in the river, good: it means purification from
>   all evils. . . .
> Seeing his face in a mirror, bad: it means another wife.
> Shod with white sandals, bad: it means roaming the earth. . . .
> His bed catching fire, bad: it means driving away his wife.

SEVEN

THE THREAT OF CHAOS

Throughout history, religion has been one way in which people have dealt with misfortune—to prevent it, to understand it, to cope with it. One of the worst misfortunes for ancient people was disease, especially because the causes were usually not understood and cures were often unknown. It seemed that illness was a form of chaos itself, resulting from the actions of hostile spirits and similar uncontrolled forces. Alternatively, people could allow chaos into their lives by acting immorally, in which case the gods might punish them with disease or other troubles. That is what the painter Neferabu believed about the blindness that had struck him:

> I am a man who swore falsely by Ptah, Lord of Truth,
> and he made me see darkness by day.
> I will declare his might to the disbeliever and the believer,

Opposite:
Blowing sand and glaring sun contributed to many eye diseases in ancient Egypt. Some blind people could find work as musicians, like this harp player.

55

to the small and the great. . . .
I being as a man who had sinned against his Lord
Righteous was Ptah, Lord of Truth, towards me
When he taught a lesson to me!

AKHENATEN'S REVOLUTION

When a commoner sinned against *maat,* the effects fell on him and his family alone. But what happened when a pharaoh, who was ultimately responsible for upholding *maat,* opened the door to chaos? According to a stela erected by Tutankhamen,

[The gods'] holy places were on the verge of disintegration,
they had become piles of rubble. . . .
The land was in grave illness,
the gods had turned their backs on this land.
If one sent soldiers to Syria,
to extend the frontiers of Egypt,
they had no success.
If one appealed to a god for succor,
he did not come.
If one besought a goddess, likewise,
she came not.
Their hearts had grown weak in their bodies,
for "they" had destroyed what had been created.

"They" were the pharaoh Akhenaten and those who had helped him close the temples of Egypt's ancient deities. Akhenaten had launched a religious revolution by rejecting all gods but Aten, the orb of the sun.

Born Amenhotep ("Amen is content"), at some point after becoming king he renamed himself Akhenaten (roughly, "Effective for Aten"). After four years on the throne, he founded a new city as his capital. He called it Akhetaten ("Horizon of Aten"; today it is known as Amarna), and he developed it as the center of worship for Aten. About five years after this, he made Aten the supreme god of Egypt, the "Sole God, who is like none other." He may not have absolutely forbidden the worship of other deities, but he certainly appears to have done his utmost to dis-

A portion of a larger-than-life statue of Akhenaten. Along with a new religion, the pharaoh promoted a new art style, in which he and his family were portrayed with exaggerated features.

courage it—he even went so far as to order the name of Amen and the word *gods* cut out of reliefs and monuments.

"There is none who knows thee save thy son Akhenaten. Thou hast made him wise in thy plans and thy power," says a hymn to Aten, almost certainly written by the king himself. In Egypt's traditional religion, priests made offerings to the gods as the pharaoh's deputies. But in the Aten religion, no priest could approach the god—only Akhenaten was fit to do so. This was one of the reasons that the Aten religion did not survive long past his death. There was no priesthood to carry it on, and there was no place at all for ordinary people in it—not even festivals to attend.

Indeed, the closing of the temples not only deprived the gods of their offerings and the priests of their livelihoods. It deprived the people of the services of the temple scribes and physicians, of the spiritual comfort of ear shrines and oracles, of the joy and excite-

AKHENATEN'S HYMN TO THE SUN

Although Akhenaten's reign was disastrous for Egypt in many ways, it did leave us some stunning pieces of art, including the beautiful poetry of the hymn that Akhenaten wrote to his god. Here are some excerpts:

How beautiful is your appearance on the horizon of heaven,
O Living Aten who creates life.
When you rise on the eastern horizon
You fill every land with your beauty.
You are beautiful and great, gleaming high over every land.
Your rays, they embrace the earth
To the furthest limits of what you have created.

. . .

Day dawns when you rise on the horizon,
You shine by day as Aten
Who dispels the darkness.
When you send forth your sunbeams
The Two Lands are festive,
The people awake and jump to their feet
For you have roused them.

. . .

The whole world goes about its work;
All cattle rest in their pastures;
Trees and vegetation are verdant;
Birds fly up from their nests, their wings raised in adoration. . .
Goats all jump to their feet and
Everything that flys and flutters lives when you shine upon it.
Boats sail upstream, and downstream likewise,
And all roads are open because you have arisen.

Akhenaten, assisted by his wife Nefertiti, worships Aten.

. . .

The earth exists in your hand, just as you have made it.
When you rise, it lives: when you set, it dies.
You yourself are Lifetime
And it is by you that men live.

ment of holidays. Not surprisingly, the common people quietly kept on worshipping their old, beloved gods. Even in Amarna itself, workers had private shrines to Isis, Hathor, Shed, Taweret, and Bes.

Akhenaten's singleminded devotion to Aten also endangered the security of Egypt's empire. When the Hittites of Asia Minor attacked Egyptian-ruled cities in what is now Syria, the king did nothing, ignoring the cities' pleas for help. To most Egyptians, foreign conquest of Egyptian territory was a sure sign that *maat* was not being upheld. Akhenaten's successors on the throne therefore looked back on his reign as a time of misery and chaos. Even as they restored the temples and monuments of the old gods, they erased the memory of the king they referred to only as "the enemy" or "that fallen foe." Within a few generations both his name and religion were forgotten, and waited till the nineteenth century to be rediscovered by archaeologists.

TROUBLES IN THE GREAT PLACE

The dishonored dead were never spoken of, but Egyptians were always exhorted to honor the blessed dead—kings, ancestors, family members, and even strangers. Outside many a tomb, carved on a stela or over a mortuary chapel's door, could be seen an inscription asking visitors and passersby to remember the deceased and leave an offering—even if the offering was only words:

> Oh you who live and exist, . . . as you love life and hate death, so shall you offer to me that which is in your hands. If there is nothing in your hands, you shall speak thus: "A thousand of bread and beer, of oxen and geese . . . a thousand of all good and pure things, for the venerated [name of the deceased]."

A woman carries offerings to a tomb or temple. Even a pharaoh's commands could not change most Egyptians' devotion to their deities and the honored dead.

The tomb of Ramses VI, showing damage done by robbers and vandals, who even managed to break the great stone sarcophagus that held the pharaoh's coffin and mummy

We would be wrong, though, if we thought that all Egyptians were completely devout. Not everyone respected the gods and the dead. In hard times people would pilfer provisions from temple storehouses. Always there were some who could not resist the temptation of the riches buried with the upper-class deceased, and many royal and noble tombs were robbed in ancient times. The thieves took anything valuable and easy to carry, in particular jewelry and amulets, as well as objects of precious metal that could be melted down for reuse. They also took useful items such as linen garments and sheets.

Toward the end of the New Kingdom, there was a rash of tomb robberies in the Valley of the Kings. Some of the robbers were caught and questioned, and the records of many cases have survived. We learn from the confessions that gangs of thieves were well organized, and usually had "inside information" from tomb workers:

> We went up in a single body. The foreigner Nesamun showed us the tomb of Ramesses VI, the Great God. We said to him, "Where is the tombmaker who was with you?" And he said to us "The cemetery worker was killed—", so he said to us. And I spent four days breaking into it [the tomb] there being five of us present. We opened the tomb and we entered it.

What made these robberies even worse was the frequently disrespectful treatment of the bodies of the dead. For example, we read, "The tombs and burial chambers in which the blessed ones of old, the male and female citizens, rest on the west of Thebes; it was found that thieves had plundered them all, dragging the owners from their inner and outer coffins and leaving them in the desert." After the end of the New Kingdom, the priests of Thebes realized that they could no longer prevent tomb robberies. Deciding to try to save at least the royal mummies, the priests took many of them from their tombs and reburied them all together in a secret place, where they stayed undiscovered and safe until the 1800s.

Since the finding of those mummies, Egyptologists have continued to make great discoveries that have taught us much about life in ancient Egypt. Perhaps the most precious remains of the ancient Egyptians, however, are their words, such as these:

I gave bread to the hungry, water to the thirsty, clothes to the naked. Never have I done anything evilly against any man. I rescued the wretched man from one who was stronger than he. . . . I was respectful to my father, pleasant to my mother. Never did I take a thing belonging to any man. Never have I said anything evilly against any person. I spoke truth. I rendered justice.

Ideally, the Egyptians tried to live their lives so that when they died, they could truthfully speak those words at the judgment of their soul. Their tombs may have been stripped of gold and treasure, but they have left us an even greater legacy in their vision of *maat* and their overwhelming love for life.

GREECE

HITTITE EMPIRE

ASIA MINOR
(ANATOLIA)

MITANNI

MESOPOTAMIA

TIGRIS RIVER

SYRIA
LEBANON

EUPHRATES RIVER

MEDITERRANEAN SEA

Megiddo ⊙

JORDAN RIVER

Babylon ⊙

LIBYA

NILE DELTA

LOWER
EGYPT

⊙ Bubastis
Giza⊙ ⊙ Heliopolis (Iunu)
Saqqara⊙⊙ ⊙ Memphis

SINAI

EGYPT

NILE RIVER

SAHARA

UPPER EGYPT

⊙ Amarna (Akhetaten)

𝕰𝕲𝕐𝕻𝕿
AND ITS NEIGHBORS
DURING THE
NEW KINGDOM

N
W E
S

Abydos ⊙

Valley of the Kings ⊙⊙ Thebes
Valley of the Queens ⊙

RED SEA

Edfu ⊙

N U B I A

MILES

0   100   200

Abu Simbel ⊙

EGYPTIAN–RULED
TERRITORY
IN THE 1400s BCE

A NOTE ON DATES, DYNASTIES, AND NAMES

The dates of the pharaohs' reigns and the spelling of their names used in this book generally follow *The Oxford History of Ancient Egypt,* edited by Ian Shaw. However, if you continue to study ancient Egypt, you will see other dates and other spellings. Here's why:

The ancient Egyptians did not calculate dates by numbering the years from a single fixed starting point as we do. Instead, they numbered the years from the beginning of each pharaoh's reign. For example, they would record events as taking place in the second year of the reign of Tutankhamen or the tenth year of the reign of Horemheb. It is often difficult to convert Egyptian dates to our dating system, so various sources give differing dates for the events of ancient Egyptian history. For this reason, all dates in this book must be considered approximate.

Scholars have traditionally divided the three thousand years of ancient Egyptian history into the following eras: the Early Dynastic Period, the Old Kingdom, the First Intermediate Period, the Middle Kingdom, the Second Intermediate Period, the New Kingdom, the Third Intermediate Period, the Late Period, and the Greco-Roman Period. The New Kingdom was comprised of three dynasties: the Eighteenth (1550–1295 BCE), Nineteenth (1295–1186 BCE), and Twentieth (1186–1069 BCE). The Eighteenth Dynasty occupies roughly the middle of ancient Egypt's history as an independent nation.

As for names, the ancient Egyptian language poses a unique set of problems. Scholars have been able to read Egyptian hieroglyphs—the famous pictures signs of ancient Egypt—since 1822. But most hieroglyphs did not stand for individual letters and their sounds, as in our alphabet. A few hieroglyphs represented single consonants, but most of them stood for groups of consonants or for entire words or concepts. Vowels were rarely indicated. These facts have made it a challenge for Egyptologists to decide on the best way to use our alphabet to spell ancient Egyptian names and words. Different spellings have been preferred at different times and places, and even today there is no agreement among scholars on exact spellings.

GLOSSARY

amulet an object felt to give magical protection, good luck, or similar qualities to the person wearing or carrying it

colonnade a line of columns, often supporting a roof over a covered walkway

electrum a mixture of silver and gold

Ennead the nine major deities whose oldest center of worship was Heliopolis: Atum (or Re or Re-Atum), Shu, Tefnut, Nut, Geb, Isis, Osiris, Nephthys, and Seth. Sometimes Horus the Elder and Horus the Younger, or other deities, were added to the Ennead; the Egyptians did not seem to mind if their group of nine actually contained more than that number.

hieroglyph a stylized picture that stood for a word, concept, group of consonants, or single consonant

hypostyle describes a structure whose roof is held up by columns or pillars

ibis a wading bird with a slender neck and long, thin, downward-curved bill. The word *ibis* comes from the Greek spelling of the bird's ancient Egyptian name, *hbw.*

inscription words written on or carved into lasting materials such as stone or metal

ka the "life force" of an individual. For deities, who might have many *ka*s, this was the part of them that could reside in a statue and make it sacred. For humans, the *ka* was one of three aspects of the soul. The

as a human-headed bird) and the *akh*. The
...nality that survived death and was able to
...ods to visit the living. The *akh* ("able spirit")
...in which the soul lived in the afterlife, sail-
...t.

lapis lazuli ... ...us stone. It had to be imported through
... ...at is now Afghanistan.

myth ... ...bout divine or semidivine beings

necropolis ... ...oup of connected cemeteries

obelisk ... ...umn with a pyramid-shaped tip (like the
Washington Monument in Washington, DC)

papyrus a reedlike plant that once grew abundantly along the Nile; a writing material made from the fibers of this plant; a document written on
this material. *Papyrus* is the source of our word *paper.*

personification a goddess, god, or other figure who stands for an abstract
quality or natural force. The god Hapy, for example, was the personification of the Nile flood.

pharaoh an ancient Egyptian king (or, occasionally, queen). The title
pharaoh—in its original form, *per aa*—for an Egyptian ruler came into
use during the New Kingdom. It initially meant "great house" and
referred to the royal palace. (Compare this to the way we sometimes say
"the White House" to mean the president.)

pylon two towers, wider at the bottom than at the top, connected in the
middle to make a huge ceremonial gateway

relief a form of sculpture in which images are carved on a flat surface,
either cut into it (sunk relief) or projecting out from it (raised relief)

scarab a kind of beetle, or a stone or other object made in the shape of a
scarab beetle

scribe a man who made his living by reading and writing. In a broader
sense, the ancient Egyptians used *scribe* to mean an educated man, one

who did not have to do manual labor but was qualified to serve in government or temple administration. A scribal education was so valued that even the highest nobles and officials proudly referred to themselves as scribes.

stela (plural, **stelae**) a stone slab or plaque carved with words and/or images to commemorate a person or event

FOR FURTHER READING

Berger, Melvin, and Gilda Berger. *Mummies of the Pharaohs: Exploring the Valley of the Kings.* Washington, DC: National Geographic, 2001.

Caselli, Giovanni. *In Search of Tutankhamun: The Discovery of a King's Tomb.* New York: Peter Bedrick, 2001.

Chrisp, Peter. *Ancient Egypt Revealed.* New York: Dorling Kindersley, 2002.

Douglas, Vincent, et al. *Illustrated Encyclopedia of Ancient Egypt.* New York: Peter Bedrick, 2001.

Green, Roger Lancelyn. *Tales of Ancient Egypt.* New York: Puffin Books, 1956 (reissued 2004).

Greenblatt, Miriam. *Hatshepsut and Ancient Egypt.* New York: Benchmark Books, 2000.

Harris, Nathaniel. *Everyday Life in Ancient Egypt.* New York: Franklin Watts, 1994.

Hart, George. *Ancient Egypt.* New York: Dorling Kindersley, 2002.

Hawass, Zahi. *Curse of the Pharaohs: My Adventures with Mummies.* Washington, DC: National Geographic, 2004.

Jovinelly, Joann, and Jason Netelkos. *The Crafts and Culture of the Ancient Egyptians.* New York: Rosen Publishing Group, 2002.

Manning, Ruth. *Ancient Egyptian Women.* Chicago: Heinemann Library, 2002.

Marston, Elsa. *The Ancient Egyptians.* New York: Benchmark Books, 1996.

Perl, Lila. *The Ancient Egyptians.* Danbury, CT: Franklin Watts, 2004.

Streissguth, Thomas. *Life in Ancient Egypt.* San Diego: Lucent Books, 2001.

ONLINE INFORMATION*

Akhet Egyptology: The Horizon to the Past.
http://www.akhet.co.uk/

The British Museum. *Ancient Egypt.*
http://www.ancientegypt.co.uk/menu.html

Carnegie Museum of Natural History. *Life in Ancient Egypt.*
    http://www.carnegiemnh.org/exhibits/egypt/guide.htm

Fleury, Kevin. *Neferchichi's Tomb.*
    http://www.neferchichi.com/index.html

Kinnaer, Jacques. *The Ancient Egypt Site.*
    http://www.ancient-egypt.org/

Metropolitan Museum of Art. *The Art of Ancient Egypt: A Web Resource.*
    http://www.metmuseum.org/explore/newegypt/htm/a_index.htm

Museum of Fine Arts. *Explore Ancient Egypt.*
    http://www.mfa.org/egypt/explore_ancient_egypt/

Nova Online. *Secrets of Lost Empires: Pharaoh's Obelisk.*
    http://www.pbs.org/wgbh/nova/lostempires/obelisk/

Odyssey Online. *Egypt.*
    http://www.carlos.emory.edu/ODYSSEY/EGYPT/homepg.html

Per-Ankh: The House of Life.
    http://www.philae.nu/PerAnkh/templepage1.html

*All Internet sites were available and accurate when this book was sent to press.

BIBLIOGRAPHY

Assmann, Jan. *The Mind of Egypt: History and Meaning in the Time of the Pharaohs.* Translated by Andrew Jenkins. New York: Metropolitan Books, 2002.

Baines, John, and Jaromír Málek. *Ancient Egypt.* Cultural Atlas of the World. Alexandria, VA: Stonehenge Press, 1984.

Editors of Time-Life Books. *Egypt: Land of the Pharaohs.* Alexandria, VA: Time-Life Books, 1992.

Fagan, Brian. *Egypt of the Pharaohs.* Washington, DC: National Geographic, 2001.

Faulkner, Raymond O., trans., et al. *The Egyptian Book of the Dead: The Book of Going Forth by Day.* Rev. ed. San Francisco: Chronicle Books, 1998.

Foster, John L., trans. *Ancient Egyptian Literature: An Anthology.* Austin: University of Texas Press, 2001.

James, T. G. H. *Pharaoh's People: Scenes from Life in Imperial Egypt.* New York: Tauris Parke Paperbacks, 2003.

Mertz, Barbara. *Red Land, Black Land: Daily Life in Ancient Egypt.* Rev. ed. New York: Dodd, Mead, 1978.

———. *Temples, Tombs and Hieroglyphs: A Popular History of Ancient Egypt.* Rev. ed. New York: Peter Bedrick Books, 1978.

Reeves, Nicholas, and Richard H. Wilkinson. *The Complete Valley of the Kings: Tombs and Treasures of Egypt's Greatest Pharaohs.* New York: Thames and Hudson, 1996.

Romer, John. *Ancient Lives: Daily Life in Egypt of the Pharaohs.* New York: Henry Holt, 1984.

Shafer, Byron E., ed. *Religion in Ancient Egypt: Gods, Myths, and Personal Practice.* Ithaca, NY: Cornell University Press, 1991.

Shaw, Ian, ed. *The Oxford History of Ancient Egypt.* Oxford: Oxford University Press, 2000.

Silverman, David P., ed. *Ancient Egypt.* New York: Oxford University Press, 1997.

Tyldesley, Joyce. *Daughters of Isis: Women of Ancient Egypt.* New York: Penguin Books, 1995.

———. *Hatchepsut: The Female Pharaoh.* New York: Penguin Books, 1996.

———. *Judgement of the Pharaoh: Crime and Punishment in Ancient Egypt.* London: Weidenfeld and Nicolson, 2000.

———. *Nefertiti: Egypt's Sun Queen.* New York: Viking, 1998.

Watterson, Barbara. *The Egyptians.* Cambridge, MA: Blackwell, 1997.

———. *Gods of Ancient Egypt.* Godalming, Surrey: Bramley Books, 1999.

White, Jon Manchip. *Everyday Life in Ancient Egypt.* New York: G. P. Putnam's Sons, 1963.

SOURCES FOR QUOTATIONS

This series of books tries to bring the ancient Egyptians to life by quoting their own words whenever possible. The quotations in this book are from the following sources:

Chapter 1: The Divine Order

p. 2 "Before the sky evolved": Silverman, *Ancient Egypt,* p. 120.

p. 2 "that which it had not known": Watterson, *Gods of Ancient Egypt,* p. 25.

p. 2 "the god who came into being": Shafer, *Religion in Ancient Egypt,* p. 110.

p. 4 "At dawn, I am called": Watterson, *Gods of Ancient Egypt,* p. 42.

p. 4 "The gods who came into being": Shafer, *Religion in Ancient Egypt,* p. 96.

p. 4 "every divine word": Watterson, *Gods of Ancient Egypt,* p. 165.

p. 5 "He is hidden": Silverman, *Ancient Egypt,* p. 127.

p. 5 "The Ennead is combined": ibid., p. 126.

p. 5 "Past knowing": Foster, *Ancient Egyptian Literature,* p. 166.

p. 6 "Lord of Time": Watterson, *Gods of Ancient Egypt,* p. 141.

Chapter 2: Temples and Tombs

p. 11 "The world fears": Watterson, *Gods of Ancient Egypt,* p. 99.

p. 11 "as though heaven": Editors of Time-Life, *Egypt,* p. 46.

p. 12 "the most select": Fagan, *Egypt of the Pharaohs,* p. 187.

p. 14 "a very great portal": Mertz, *Red Land, Black Land,* p. 272.

p. 18 "O shabti": Faulkner, *The Egyptian Book of the Dead,* p. 101.

Chapter 3: Priests

p. 22 "Lord of the Master Craftsmen": Silverman, *Ancient Egypt,* p. 165.

p. 22 "Greatest of Seers": Mertz, *Red Land, Black Land,* p. 272.

p. 22 "Come to your body": Silverman, *Ancient Egypt,* p. 151.

p. 24 "I was a truthful witness": from J. H. Breasted, *Ancient Records of Egypt,* available
online at http://nefertiti.iwebland.com/texts/bekenkhonsu.htm

p. 25 "86,486 serfs": Watterson, *Gods of Ancient Egypt,* p. 142.

p. 26 "voice of the heart": Mertz, *Red Land, Black Land,* p. 241.

p. 27 "a woman skilled": Watterson, *Gods of Ancient Egypt,* p. 41.

p. 27 "the god's words": Faulkner, *The Egyptian Book of the Dead,* p. 147.

p. 27 "The first spell": Silverman, *Ancient Egypt,* p. 101.

Chapter 4: Women and Religion

p. 30 "Holy music for Hathor": Tyldesley, *Daughters of Isis,* p. 129.

p. 31 "every day": ibid., p. 129.

p. 31 "The Principal Wife": Tyldesley, *Nefertiti,* p. 24.

p. 32 "Amen, Lord of Thrones": Tyldesley, *Daughters of Isis,* p. 221.

p. 33 "See her": Foster, *Ancient Egyptian Literature,* p. 101.

Chapter 5: From Birth to Death and Beyond

p. 37 "May a birth": Silverman, *Ancient Egypt,* p. 85.

p. 37 "Hathor, remember": Romer, *Ancient Lives,* p. 28.

p. 38 "Gift of Amen": Tyldesley, *Daughters of Isis,* p. 77.

p. 38 "Perish, you who come": ibid., p. 79.

p. 40 "O my heart": Tyldesley, *Judgement of the Pharaoh,* p. 169.

p. 41 "I have judged the heart" and "The vindicated Osiris": Faulkner, *The Egyptian Book
of the Dead,* plate 3.

p. 42 "for his sake": Foster, *Ancient Egyptian Literature,* p. 104.

p. 42 "His sister served": ibid., p. 106.

p. 42 "May your arms": Romer, *Ancient Lives,* p. 30.

Chapter 6: Holidays and Every Day

p. 45 "the mayor Mentuhotpe greets": James, *Pharaoh's People,* pp. 174–175.

p. 46 "You are Amen": Tyldesley, *Daughters of Isis,* p. 246.

p. 47 "There was nobody": Watterson, *Gods of Ancient Egypt,* p. 208.

p. 48 "Become an *akh*": Silverman, *Ancient Egypt,* p. 153.

p. 48 "Memphis and every city": Shaw, *The Oxford History of Ancient Egypt,* p. 247.

p. 51 "Rejoicing in heaven": Assmann, *The Mind of Egypt,* p. 232.

p. 52 "Sit on your throne": Watterson, *Gods of Ancient Egypt,* p. 43.

p. 52 "Cause your eye" and "I have prevailed": Shafer, *Religion in Ancient Egypt,* p. 110.

p. 52 "How good": ibid., pp. 110–111.

p. 52 "She drank": ibid., p. 111.

p. 53 "I shall give you": Shaw, *The Oxford History of Ancient Egypt,* p. 247.

p. 53 "If a man sees": Silverman, *Ancient Egypt,* p. 100.

Chapter 7: The Threat of Chaos

p. 55 "I am a man": Romer, *Ancient Lives,* p. 104.

p. 56 "[The gods'] holy places": Assmann, *The Mind of Egypt,* pp. 223–224.

p. 57 "Sole God": Watterson, *Gods of Ancient Egypt,* p. 160.

p. 57 "There is none": Fagan, *Egypt of the Pharaohs,* p. 207.

p. 58 "How beautiful": Watterson, *Gods of Ancient Egypt,* pp. 159–162.

p. 59 "Oh you who live": Mertz, *Red Land, Black Land,* p. 347.

p. 60 "We went up": Romer, *Ancient Lives,* p. 180.

p. 61 "The tombs and burial chambers": Tyldesley, *Judgement of the Pharaoh,* p. 134.

p. 61 "I gave bread": Mertz, *Red Land, Black Land,* p. 363.

INDEX

ABOUT THE AUTHOR

When Kathryn Hinds was in sixth grade, she wanted to be an Egyptologist more than anything. Eventually she discovered that her true calling was writing, but she still loves archaeology and ancient history. She has written a number of books for young people about premodern cultures, including the books in the series LIFE IN THE ROMAN EMPIRE, LIFE IN THE RENAISSANCE, and LIFE IN THE MIDDLE AGES. Kathryn lives in the north Georgia mountains with her husband, their son, and an assortment of cats and dogs. When she is not writing, she enjoys spending time with her family and friends, reading, dancing, playing music, gardening, knitting, and taking walks in the woods.

Fox Gradin, Celestial Studios Photography